WHY CHEMISTRY MATTERS

ATOMS AND
MOLECULES

MOLLY
ALOIAN

Crabtree Publishing Company

www.crabtreebooks.com

Crabtree Publishing Company
www.crabtreebooks.com

Author: Molly Aloian
Coordinating editor: Chester Fisher
Series editor: Scholastic Ventures
Project manager: Santosh Vasudevan (Q2AMEDIA)
Art direction: Dibakar Acharjee (Q2AMEDIA)
Cover design: Ranjan Singh (Q2AMEDIA)
Design: Tarang Saggar (Q2AMEDIA)
Photo research: Anju Pathak (Q2AMEDIA)
Editor: Adrianna Morganelli
Proofreader: Reagan Miller
Project coordinator: Robert Walker
Production coordinator: Katherine Berti
Font management: Mike Golka
Prepress technicians: Samara Parent, Ken Wright

Photographs:
Cover: Nat Ulrich/Shutterstock, Q2A Artwork (inset); Title page: Radu Razvan/Romania/123RF; P4: Alex Staroseltsev/Shutterstock; P5: Mike Norton/Istockphoto (top), Library of Congress Prints and Photographs (bottom); P6: Chepe Nicoli/Shutterstock; P7: Gualtier Boffi/Shutterstock; P11: John R. Kreul/IPS/CFWImages.com/Photographersdirect (top); P11: Ken Lucas/Getty Images (bottom); P12: Pilar Echevarria/Shutterstock; P13: Pinfoldphotos/Dreamstime; P14: Sylada/Dreamstime; P15: Xmmx/Shutterstock; P16: Zoomteam/Dreamstime; P17: Achim Prill/Istockphoto; P18: Image Source/Jupiter Images; P19: Riccardo Bastianello/Shutterstock; P20: The Print Collector/Alamy; P21: Library of Congress Prints and Photographs; P22: Library of Congress Prints and Photographs; P23: Luca Medical/Alamy; P24: Eraxion/Dreamstime; P25: Yann Forget/Wikipedia; P26: Dan Collier/Shutterstock; P27: Natalia Bratslavsky/Shutterstock; P29: Jane Bernard/Associated Press

Library and Archives Canada Cataloguing in Publication

Aloian, Molly
    Atoms and molecules / Molly Aloian.

(Why chemistry matters)
Includes index.
ISBN 978-0-7787-4240-1 (bound).--ISBN 978-0-7787-4247-0 (pbk.)

    1. Atoms--Juvenile literature. 2. Molecules--Juvenile literature.
3. Matter--Constitution--Juvenile literature. I. Title. II. Series.

QC173.16.A46 2008   j539'.1   C2008-903651-4

Library of Congress Cataloging-in-Publication Data

Aloian, Molly.
    Atoms and molecules / Molly Aloian.
      p. cm. -- (Why chemistry matters)
    Includes index.
    ISBN-13: 978-0-7787-4247-0 (pbk. : alk. paper)
    ISBN-10: 0-7787-4247-4 (pbk. : alk. paper)
    ISBN-13: 978-0-7787-4240-1 (reinforced lib. bdg. : alk. paper)
    ISBN-10: 0-7787-4240-7 (reinforced lib. bdg. : alk. paper)
    1. Atoms--Juvenile literature. 2. Molecules--Juvenile literature. 3. Matter--Constitution--Juvenile literature. I. Title. II. Series.

QC173.16.A56 2009
539.7--dc22

2008025367

Crabtree Publishing Company

www.crabtreebooks.com   1-800-387-7650

Printed in the USA/032014/JA20140203

Published in Canada
Crabtree Publishing
616 Welland Ave.
St. Catharines, ON
L2M 5V6

Published in the United States
Crabtree Publishing
PMB 59051
350 Fifth Avenue, 59th Floor
New York, New York 10118

Published in the United Kingdom
Crabtree Publishing
Maritime House
Basin Road North, Hove
BN41 1WR

Published in Australia
Crabtree Publishing
3 Charles Street
Coburg North
VIC, 3058

Contents

Atoms and Molecules

For centuries, people have wondered about the things they see around them such as trees, rocks, and water. People wondered about the particles inside the materials. How were they the same? How were they different? People could not easily answer these questions, but as time passed, scientists made amazing discoveries about the world around them and the materials in it.

What is the smallest thing you can think of? Is it a single grain of salt? Is it a single grain of sand? Though hard to believe, smaller things exist on Earth. Tiny particles called atoms form every grain of salt and every grain of sand. Atoms are among the smallest things on Earth. All **matter** on Earth is composed of atoms. Matter is a substance that occupies space and has **mass**. Mass is related to weight, which is the pull of **gravity** on the object. Trees, rocks, water, and even air are all composed of matter.

Atoms are too small for people to see. Scientists cannot see them even through a powerful microscope! There are billions of atoms in the tiniest grain of salt or sand.

Trees, rocks, air, and water are all composed of matter.

Atoms do not change. For example, a gold ring contains only gold atoms and they are all the same. You can melt the gold or grind the gold into dust, but what is left will still contain only gold atoms. Atoms do not change, but they join with other atoms. Some atoms join with other atoms and form **molecules**.

Ice, water, and steam all have the same molecules of hydrogen and oxygen.

Atomic Theory

In 1807, a British chemist named John Dalton presented his atomic theory. He introduced the word "atom" in this theory. Two of the main ideas of this theory are that there are tiny particles in matter and that atoms cannot be made, destroyed, or divided. Later, Dalton proposed that atoms could split into even smaller particles. Scientists eventually proved Dalton right.

John Dalton's atomic theory changed science forever.

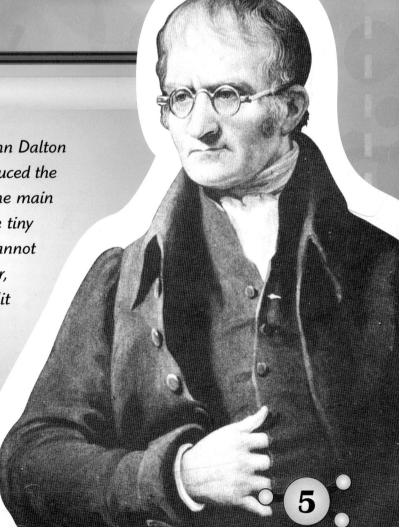

Subatomic Particles

For nearly 100 years, people accepted John Dalton's ideas about the atom. But, starting in the 1890s, scientists made a series of new discoveries. They discovered that they could divide the atom into even smaller particles called **protons**, **neutrons**, and **electrons**. Protons, neutrons, and electrons are **subatomic particles**, or particles that are part of an atom. Protons and electrons have electrical charges. Protons are positively charged and electrons are negatively charged. Neutrons have no electrical charge; they are neutral. Particles with opposite electrical charges attract each other. This means that a positively charged proton attracts a negatively charged electron and **repels** another positive charge. A negatively charged electron attracts a positively charged proton and repels another negative charge.

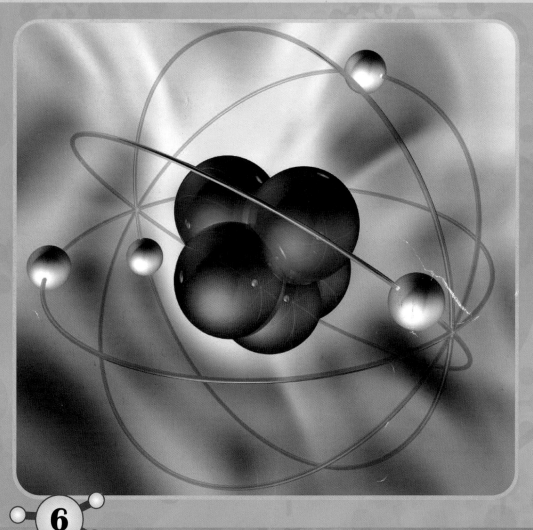

These electrons orbit around the nucleus of an atom. The nucleus is the central part of the atom.

Each atom has a **nucleus** in the middle. The atom's nucleus occupies a very small part of the atom. Protons and neutrons form the nucleus. Protons and neutrons are about the same size. The neutron has slightly more mass, however. Electrons spin around the nucleus at very great distances from it. Electrons are smaller than protons and neutrons. They have a much smaller mass than protons. In an atom, the number of electrons is usually the same as the number of protons.

Ions

*Atoms usually have the same number of protons and electrons. The positive charges in the protons and the negative charges in the electrons cancel each other out. So the atom is neutral and has no charge. This is not the case with **ions**. Ions form when an atom gains or loses one or more electrons. An ion is either an **anion** or a **cation**.*

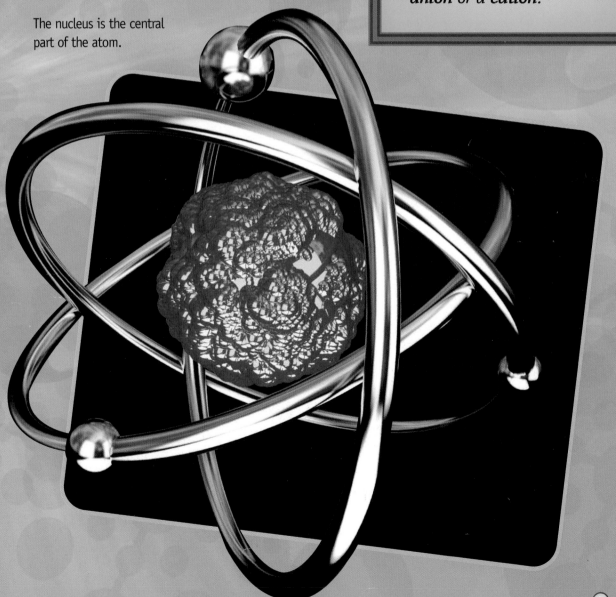

The nucleus is the central part of the atom.

Energy in Electrons

An electron orbiting far from the nucleus contains more energy than an electron that is close to the nucleus. Some electrons have the same amount of energy. Electrons that have the same amount of energy have the same energy level. They orbit approximately the same distance from the nucleus. Every atom has seven levels of energy.

Some models show electrons with the same amount of energy circling the nucleus at the same energy level. Scientists often call the level a **shell**. In the models, each shell only holds a certain number of electrons before it becomes full. A shell must contain its maximum number of electrons before any other electrons can appear in the shells outside it.

The number of electrons and shells in an atom affects the way it reacts with other atoms. An atom with shells that are not full is more likely to be **reactive** than one with full shells. A reactive atom is able to gain or lose the electrons it needs to **bond**, or join, with another atom. The more reactive an atom is, the more easily it bonds.

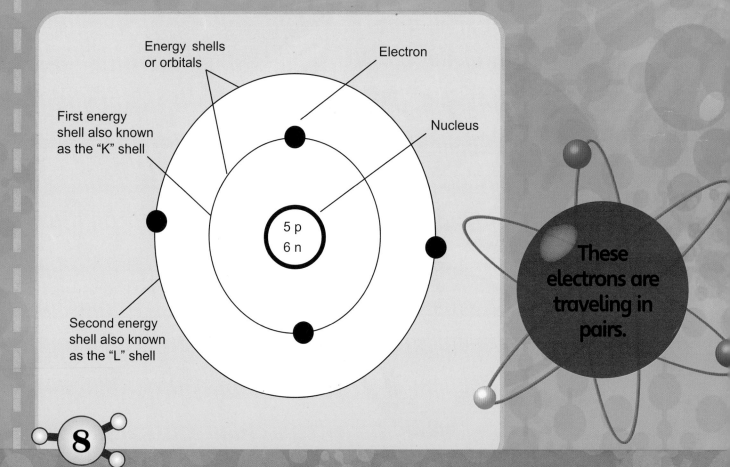

Energy shells or orbitals

Electron

First energy shell also known as the "K" shell

Nucleus

5 p
6 n

Second energy shell also known as the "L" shell

These electrons are traveling in pairs.

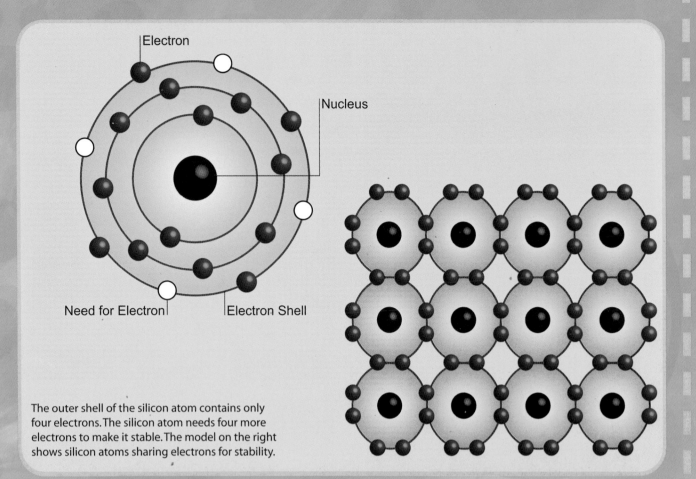

Electron

Nucleus

Need for Electron

Electron Shell

The outer shell of the silicon atom contains only four electrons. The silicon atom needs four more electrons to make it stable. The model on the right shows silicon atoms sharing electrons for stability.

The shell model helps scientists understand atoms, but scientists know that real atoms do not look like they do in the model.

By exposing them to heat or light, electrons gain energy and become excited. They use this energy to jump from one shell to another shell that is farther from the nucleus. Electrons use most of the energy in the jump and then fall back to their original shells. Remember! The farther a shell is from the nucleus, the more energy its electrons contain.

Two of a Kind

*Electrons often move in pairs. Both electrons are negatively charged. But they do not repel each other because they spin in opposite directions while they circle around the nucleus. One electron spins one way and the other electron spins the other way. The paths that the electrons take are **orbitals**. An orbital contains two electrons.*

The Nucleus

The nucleus contains neutrons and positively charged protons. Some scientists believe that an atom would fall apart if there were no neutrons in the nucleus. Protons all have the same electrical charge, so they want to repel each other. Neutrons keep the protons in place. The more protons there are in a nucleus, the stronger the electrical charge.

The number of protons in an atom is its atomic number. Hydrogen has an atomic number of one because it has only one proton in the nucleus. Remember that the number of protons equals the number of electrons in a nucleus. Carbon has six protons and six electrons orbiting the nucleus, so its atomic number is six.

A nucleus can **decay** if it becomes **unstable**. The nucleus of an atom with an **atomic number** higher than 83 has so many protons and neutrons that it becomes unstable. It begins to break up. In an unstable nucleus, a neutron can break up into a proton, an electron, and even smaller particles. As an atom breaks up, the nucleus becomes **radioactive**, which means it gives off **radiation**. Radiation is energy given off in the form of waves or particles. It can harm living things, including human beings. Read more about the three types of radiation on pages 20-21.

Mass Number

*Atoms come in many sizes. The protons and neutrons in an atom determine an atom's mass. The number of protons and neutrons an atom contains is its **mass number**. Electrons add very little to the total mass of an atom, so the mass number does not include their weight. An atom's mass number is the mass of its nucleus.*

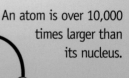

An atom is over 10,000 times larger than its nucleus.

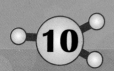

More uranium is mined in Canada than any other country.

Uranium has 92 protons, 92 electrons, and 146 neutrons. Its mass number is 238.

Elements

An **element** is a substance made from just one kind of atom. Each atom in an element has the same number of protons. Iron, copper, helium, hydrogen, and oxygen are examples of some elements. Different elements have different atomic numbers. An element's atomic number helps identify the element. For example, there are 11 protons in a sodium atom so its atomic number is 11. Sodium is the only element with this atomic number.

There are about 100 different elements. They can combine with each other to create every substance on Earth. There are about 90 elements that occur naturally on Earth, including the gold and silver in jewelry, the oxygen found in air, the aluminum in foil, and the copper in pennies. Scientists created the other elements. They made a chart of all the elements. It is the Periodic Table of Elements. The table lists the elements in order of how many protons they have.

Metals, such as the copper in this pot, are good conductors of heat and electricity.

Periodic Table of Elements

| 1.0 |
| H |
| hydrogen |
| 1 |

Key
relative atomic mass
atomic number
name
atomic (proton) number

| (18) |
| 4.0 |
| He |
| helium |
| 2 |

(1)	(2)	(3)	(4)	(5)	(6)	(7)	(8)	(9)	(10)	(11)	(12)	(13)	(14)	(15)	(16)	(17)	
6.9	9.0											10.8	12.0	14.0	16.0	19.0	20.2
Li	Be											B	C	N	O	F	Ne
lithium	beryllium											boron	carbon	nitrogen	oxygen	fluorine	neon
3	4											5	6	7	8	9	10
23.0	24.3											27.0	28.1	31.0	32.1	35.5	39.9
Na	Mg											Al	Si	P	S	Cl	Ar
sodium	magnesium											aluminium	silicon	phosphorus	sulphur	chlorine	argon
11	12											13	14	15	16	17	18
39.1	40.1	45.0	47.9	50.9	52.0	54.9	55.8	58.9	58.7	63.5	65.4	69.7	72.6	74.9	79.0	79.9	83.8
K	Ca	Sc	Ti	V	Cr	Mn	Fe	Co	Ni	Cu	Zn	Ga	Ge	As	Se	Br	Kr
potassium	calcium	scandium	titanium	vanadium	chromium	manganese	iron	cobalt	nickel	copper	zinc	gallium	germanium	arsenic	selenium	bromine	krypton
19	20	21	22	23	24	25	26	27	28	29	30	31	32	33	34	35	36
85.5	87.6	88.9	91.2	92.9	95.9	98.9	101.1	102.9	106.4	107.9	112.4	114.8	118.7	121.8	127.6	126.9	131.3
Rb	Sr	Y	Zr	Nb	Mo	Tc	Ru	Rh	Pd	Ag	Cd	In	Sn	Sb	Te	I	Xe
rubidium	strontium	yttrium	zirconium	niobium	molybdenum	technetium	ruthenium	rhodium	palladium	silver	cadmium	indium	tin	antimony	tellurium	iodine	xenon
37	38	39	40	41	42	43	44	45	46	47	48	49	50	51	52	53	54
132.9	137.3	138.9	178.5	180.9	183.9	186.2	190.2	192.2	195.1	197.0	200.6	204.4	207.2	209.0	210.0	210.0	222.0
Cs	Ba	La *	Hf	Ta	W	Re	Os	Ir	Pt	Au	Hg	Tl	Pb	Bi	Po	At	Rn
caesium	barium	lanthanum	hafnium	tantalum	tungsten	rhenium	osmium	iridium	platinum	gold	mercury	thallium	lead	bismuth	polonium	astatine	radon
55	56	57	72	73	74	75	76	77	78	79	80	81	82	83	84	85	86
[223.0]	[226.0]	[227]	[261]	[262]	[266]	[264]	[277]	[268]	[271]	[272]							
Fr	Ra	Ac †	Rf	Db	Sg	Bh	Hs	Mt	Ds	Rg							
francium	radium	actinium	rutherfordium	dubnium	seaborgium	bohnium	hassium	meitnerium	darmstadium	roentgenium							
87	88	89	104	105	106	107	108	109	110	111							

Elements with atomic numbers 112-116 have been reported
but not fully authenticad

* 58 – 71 Lanthanides

140.1	140.9	144.2	144.9	150.4	152.0	157.3	158.9	162.5	164.9	167.3	168.9	173.0	175.0
Ce	Pr	Nd	Pm	Sm	Eu	Gd	Tb	Dy	Ho	Er	Tm	Yb	Lu
cerium	praseodymium	neodymium	promethium	samarium	europium	gadolinium	terbium	dysprosium	holmium	erbium	thulium	ytterbium	lutetium
58	59	60	61	82	63	64	65	66	67	68	69	70	71

† 90 – 103 Actinides

232.0	231.0	238.0	237.0	239.1	243.1	247.1	247.1	252.1	[252]	[257]	[258]	[259]	[260]
Th	Pa	U	Np	Pu	Am	Cm	Bk	Cf	Es	Fm	Md	No	Lr
thorium	protactinium	uranium	neptunium	plutonium	americium	curium	berkelium	californium	einsteinium	fermium	mendelevium	nobelium	lawrencium
90	91	92	93	94	95	96	97	98	99	100	101	102	103

Hydrogen is the lightest element. It is the most abundant element in the universe.

Metals, nonmetals, and metalloids are three types of elements. Over half of all elements are metals. Gold is a metal. There are 16 nonmetals. The most commonly used nonmetals are in the form of gas. Helium is a gas. People fill balloons with helium to make them float because helium is lighter than air. There are seven metalloids. Metalloids are not metals or nonmetals, but they can have characteristics of metals or nonmetals. Silicon is a metalloid. Computer microchips contain silicon.

Physical and Chemical Properties

Elements are grouped together according to their **physical properties** and **chemical properties**. Color, scent, and **state of matter** are some physical properties. State of matter refers to whether something is a liquid, a solid, or a gas. Grape juice is purple and smells sweet. It is a liquid. These are all physical properties. A material's reaction with something else is its chemical property. Wood burns in air. This is a chemical property.

Chemical Reactions

Elements combine to make most everything on Earth. When elements combine, **chemical reactions** take place. Chemical reactions are changes that produce one or more new substances. Burning, changes in color, and bubbles of gas in liquid are all chemical reactions. These reactions create new substances called **compounds.** Compounds have different properties than the substances from which they came. Sodium chloride is a compound. It forms when sodium and chlorine react. If a person ate pure sodium or inhaled chlorine, he or she would become very sick. But people eat sodium chloride all the time. It is table salt.

Two Types of Compounds

*There are two types of compounds: **covalent compounds** and **ionic compounds.** Covalent compounds have atoms of different elements that share electrons. Sharing electrons bonds the atoms together to form new molecules. Water is an example of a covalent compound. When a metal atom loses an electron to a nonmetal atom, an ionic compound is formed. Salt is an example of an ionic compound.*

Common table salt is the result of a chemical reaction between sodium and chlorine.

Compounds contain elements combined in very specific ways. Water is a compound that is composed of two hydrogen atoms and one oxygen atom. If only one hydrogen atom combines with one oxygen atom, the compound is not water. Compounds can only be separated with chemical reactions, too. Heating the compound sugar causes it to break up into carbon, hydrogen, and water.

Mixtures are different substances—elements or compounds—mixed together without a chemical reaction taking place. Forming a mixture is a physical change, not a chemical change. Mixtures usually keep the same properties as the original substances from which they came. Unlike compounds, you can make a mixture in many ways. For example, there can be any amount of salt and water in a mixture of salt water. You can separate the ingredients in a mixture without a chemical reaction. Physical bonds hold ingredients together, not chemical bonds.

Iron reacts with water and oxygen in the air. The chemical reaction is causing this car to slowly rust.

States of Matter

A physical change is a change in the state of matter. Solids, liquids, and gases are all different states of matter. When a substance changes from one state of matter to another, the temperature of its molecules must increase or decrease. Molecules get warmer and gain energy if the temperature increases. They also move faster. Molecules get cooler and lose energy if the temperature decreases. They move more slowly. Changes in states of matter are physical changes, not chemical changes.

The molecules in solids, such as pieces of wood, are packed tightly together. They move very little and their shape does not change easily. The molecules in liquids and gases are not as tightly bound to one another. The molecules are farther apart and they can move from their positions. The molecules in gases can move freely. **Kinetic energy** is the energy of motion. A molecule's kinetic energy is the energy it possesses because of its movement.

In cold temperatures, water molecules get cooler. They freeze and turn into ice.

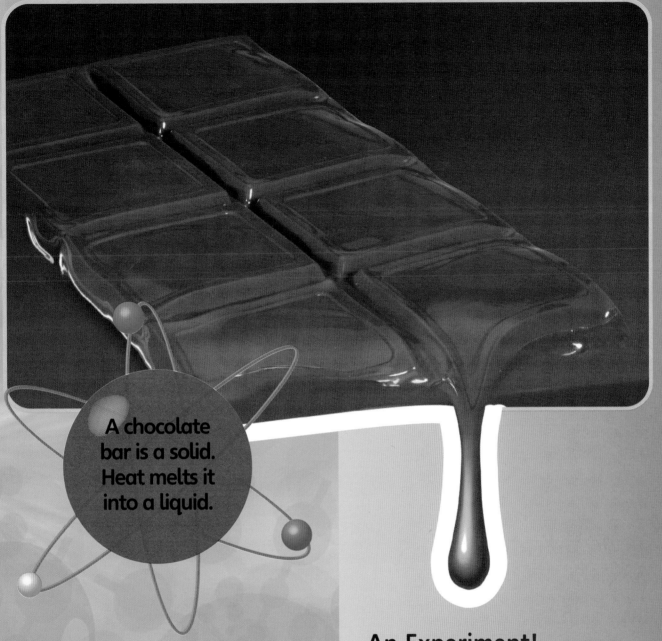

A chocolate bar is a solid. Heat melts it into a liquid.

There are two other states of matter: plasmas and Bose-Einstein condensates. These states of matter exist at extreme temperatures. Plasmas require extremely hot temperatures in order to form. Plasma is a gas made of flowing ions and electrons, which conduct electricity. It is the most common state of matter in the universe. Bose-Einstein condensates are the opposite of plasmas. They form at extremely low temperatures when atoms fuse together.

An Experiment!

Pour exactly one cup of water into a glass measuring cup. Make sure that the water is right at the one cup (250 mL) line. Add one heaping spoonful of salt and dissolve it in the water. You will see that the salt did not raise the water level. The salt molecules fit in between the loose water molecules.

Electricity

Flowing electrons form the energy called electricity. If you rub a balloon against a wool sweater for a long time, the balloon will stick to the wall. Rubbing creates a type of electricity commonly known as static electricity. Rubbing causes electrons to pull from the surface of one material and transfer to the surface of the other material. The wool sweater loses electrons and ends up with an excess of positively charged particles. The balloon gains electrons and ends up with an excess of negatively charged particles on its surface. The balloon sticks to the wall because the wall does not have an excess of either charge.

Static electricity can also cause your hair to stand on end. If a person wears a wool hat and takes it off, the hat rubs against his or her hair. Negatively charged electrons move from the hair to the hat. As a result, each strand of hair has a positive charge and the positive charges repel each other. Each hair stands up and away from the others.

The Davy Lamp

*Humphry Davy invented a safety light for **miners** called the Davy lamp. Miners used the lamp in place of open flames such as candles. Gases often build up in coal mines, and open flames sometimes caused the gases to explode. The Davy lamp did not **ignite** the gases as candles did. Davy's invention saved hundreds of miners' lives!*

This girl has positively charged particles repelling each other in her hair. Her hairs are trying to get away from each other!

In 1799, British chemist Humphry Davy discovered **electrolysis**. By passing an electrical **current**, or stream of electrical charge, through compounds, Davy discovered that they could separate into their component elements. For example, passing a mild electric current through water separated the liquid into hydrogen and oxygen. The hydrogen and oxygen also changed to gases. Davy used electrolysis to separate other substances and discovered new elements, such as potassium and sodium.

This storm cloud is charged with static electricity. The American inventor Benjamin Franklin showed that lightning was static electricity.

Radiation

What is radiation and how does it develop? When an atom's nucleus is unstable, it is likely to fall apart. Uranium is an example of an unstable element. Uranium has the mass number 235. It has 92 protons, 92 electrons, and 143 neutrons. This uranium is not radioactive, but an **isotope** of uranium, called uranium 238, is radioactive. It has three extra neutrons. An isotope is a different form of an atom of the same element. It has the same number of protons, but a different number of neutrons. Most elements have isotopes. One isotope is sometimes more unstable than another isotope of the same element. Unstable isotopes are radioactive.

Radioactivity is the particles given off when unstable atoms decay into smaller, more stable atoms. The atom becomes stable or non-radioactive when it has given off all its radioactive particles. Radiation can occur naturally, or scientists can create it in laboratories. Radiation can help people, such as in medicine or creating energy. But it can also harm living things.

Marie Curie worked with her husband Pierre to extract tiny amounts of radioactive materials for her to study.

Ernest Rutherford

Physicist Ernest Rutherford conducted famous experiments on atoms and radioactivity. The discoveries made by Marie Curie about radiation provided Rutherford with insight into the structure of the atom. The particles given off by radioactive substances led Rutherford to discover that every atom contains a positively charged nucleus. He made this discovery in 1911.

Henri Becquerel was born into a family of scholars and scientists.

In 1896, French physicist Antoine Henri Becquerel accidentally discovered radioactivity. The next year, French physicist Marie Curie began to research the subject of radiation. Curie discovered radium and polonium, two important radioactive elements. She won the Nobel Prize for Physics in 1903 and the Nobel Prize for Chemistry in 1911. She died from a type of cancer in 1934. The exposure to radiation most likely caused her cancer.

Types of Radiation

In 1900, Ernest Rutherford discovered three different types of radiation: alpha particles, beta particles, and gamma rays. An alpha particle has two protons and two neutrons. A beta particle has the charge and the mass of an electron. A beta particle travels faster and farther than an alpha particle does. It is also smaller than an alpha particle. Gamma rays travel farther than beta particles and can pass right through solid objects.

People first used radiation to treat certain types of cancer. Cancer cells often cause tumors in the body. People use radiation to change the subatomic particles in cancer cells and make them harmless. But exposure to too much radiation can cause cancer. So doctors must perform radiation treatment without damaging healthy cells. The radioactive substance people most commonly use to treat cancer is cobalt-60.

Radiation can also follow a substance through a person's bloodstream. This is called **tracing**. For example, a doctor can discover how a patient's body reacts to sugar with carbon-14. The patient eats the sugar combined with carbon-14, and doctors follow the path of the sugar through the patient's body by using a Geiger counter. A Geiger counter is a special device that detects radioactive particles.

Ernest Rutherford researched radiation at Cambridge University, in England.

Carbon Dating

All living things contain a small amount of carbon-14.
When a living thing dies, the amount of carbon-14 slowly
decreases. The carbon-14 is not replaced. Carbon dating is a
way of determining the age of objects up to about 50,000
years old. Carbon dating can determine the age of bone,
cloth, wood, and plant fibers from the past. **Archaeologists**
measure the amount of carbon-14 to find the object's age.

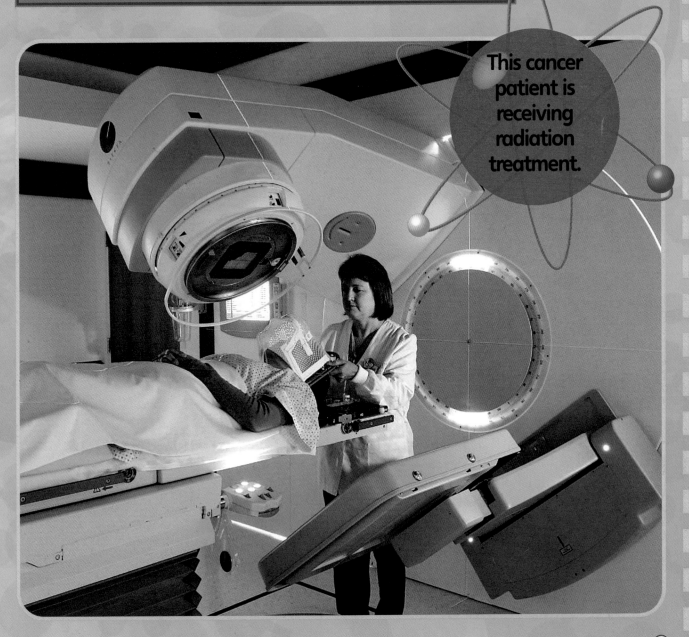

This cancer patient is receiving radiation treatment.

Nuclear Fission

People use radiation most commonly in nuclear power stations to create electricity. A nuclear reaction is the process of creating radiation. One type of nuclear reaction is **nuclear fission**. Nuclear fission is changing atoms by splitting apart their nuclei. When an atom splits, there is an explosive burst of heat, light, and radiation.

Scientists Otto Hahn and Lise Meitner discovered nuclear fission. It can occur naturally in large, unstable nuclei. It can also occur in a machine called a **particle accelerator**. A particle accelerator looks like a very long canon. Using huge amounts of energy, it fires subatomic particles at each other. As the particles smash together, they explode into smaller particles. Uranium was one of the first elements to have its atoms split.

An atomic bomb is a nuclear weapon. A nuclear weapon is the most destructive weapon ever created.

Discoveries by Ernest Rutherford and Marie Curie led to the belief that atoms would produce enormous amounts of energy when they broke apart. Scientist Albert Einstein was scared that Germans were going to use the fission process to make a new kind of bomb. He pushed the United States government to develop one first. The atomic bomb, first used in World War II, demonstrated the energy that breaking atoms apart produced. In 1945, the United States dropped atomic bombs on the Japanese cities of Hiroshima and Nagasaki, causing much death and destruction.

This picture shows a nuclear power station. Creating and operating a nuclear power station is a very complex process.

Nuclear Power Stations

*There are hundreds of nuclear power stations in the world. The reactions take place in the core of the nuclear power station. In the core, radioactive materials provide fuel. The fuel creates nuclear energy, which creates steam. Steam turns a **turbine**, which generates electricity. Nuclear power stations supply more than one quarter of the world's supply of electricity.*

Nuclear Fusion

Another type of nuclear reaction is called **nuclear fusion**. This occurs when two nuclei are forced together to create a larger, heavier nucleus. The bonding of the nuclei releases energy. High temperatures and huge pressure are both required in order for nuclear fusion to take place. Nuclear fusion and fission both take place in another type of bomb, called a hydrogen bomb. A hydrogen bomb contains an atomic bomb powered by fission. A substance containing hydrogen surrounds the bomb. The energy created by fission causes the hydrogen nuclei to fuse together to create helium atoms.

The Sun is a star. Nuclear fusion powers all stars, including the Sun. The fusion converts hydrogen into helium atoms. Nuclear fusion is the source of all the heat and light energy pouring out of the Sun.

Nuclear fusion works best with two heavier isotopes of hydrogen. The isotopes are called deuterium and tritium. Deuterium has one proton and one neutron. Tritium has one proton and two neutrons. Fusing the nucleus of deuterium and the nucleus of tritium creates helium. Helium is an alpha particle. When the two nuclei fuse, the extra neutron and an enormous surge of energy are released.

Nuclear fusion is constantly taking place within the Sun.

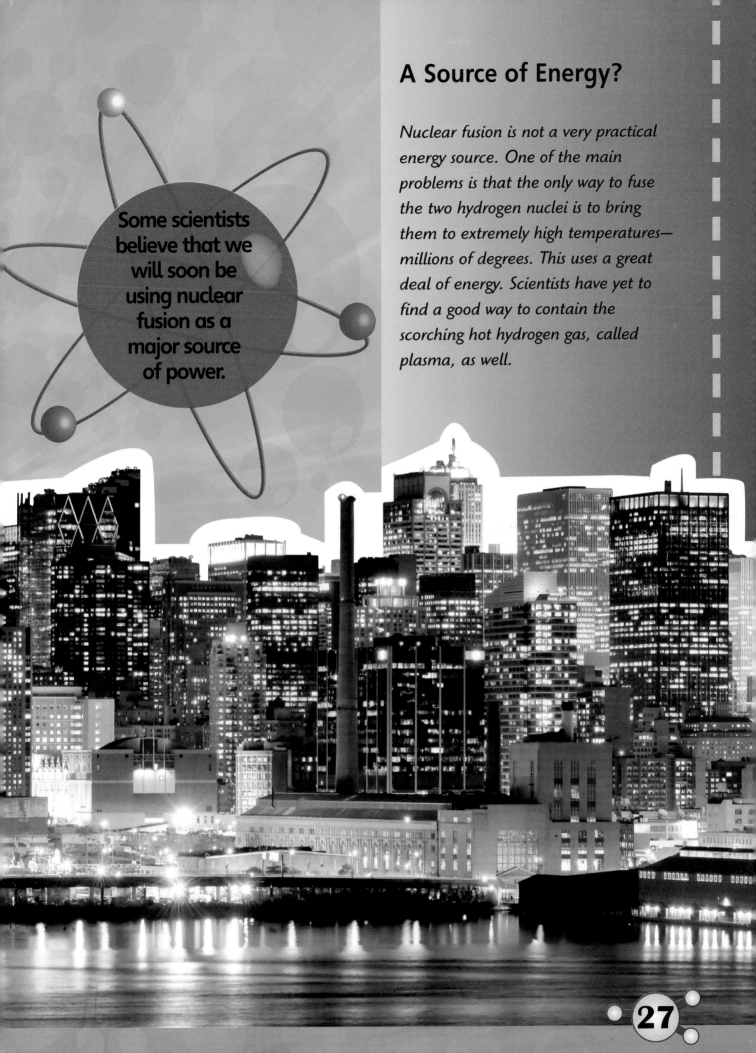

A Source of Energy?

Nuclear fusion is not a very practical energy source. One of the main problems is that the only way to fuse the two hydrogen nuclei is to bring them to extremely high temperatures—millions of degrees. This uses a great deal of energy. Scientists have yet to find a good way to contain the scorching hot hydrogen gas, called plasma, as well.

Some scientists believe that we will soon be using nuclear fusion as a major source of power.

Quarks

In 1963, American physicist Murray Gell-Mann proposed that protons and neutrons consist of more fundamental particles. He called these particles **quarks**. There are six types of quarks: top, bottom, up, down, charm, and strange. Scientists discovered that each quark has its own mass and electrical charge. They described the differences in these properties with the word "flavor." For example, quarks have either up, down, or strange flavor. Flavors are ways to identify the different kinds of quarks.

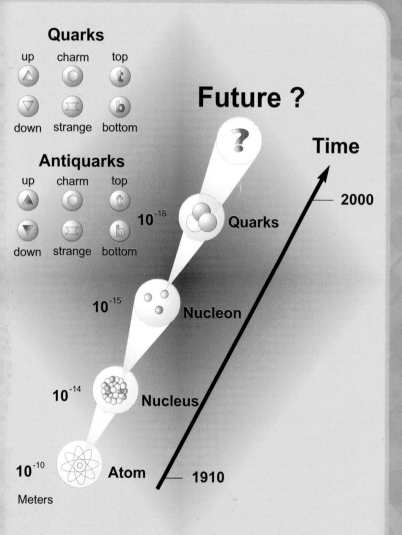

Quarks

up   charm   top

down   strange   bottom

Antiquarks

up   charm   top

down   strange   bottom

Future ?

Time

2000

10^{-18} Quarks

10^{-15} Nucleon

10^{-14} Nucleus

10^{-10} Atom

1910

Meters

Scientists also decided that each flavor can come in three different forms, called colors. The colors are a way of classifying quarks according to the way they join with other quarks. There are different sets of color names. For example, red, blue, and green is a popular set of quark colors. Quark colors can attract or repel each other, but they have **fractional**, or fairly small, electric charges. Some scientists believe that quarks hold together in particles by color force. Color force is the force between quarks. Another particle, called a gluon, carries the force and glues the quarks together. No one has seen a quark, but experiments and theories suggest that they exist. People cannot detect the quarks themselves, but quarks quickly decay into other particles that people can detect.

Protons and neutrons are combinations of three quarks.

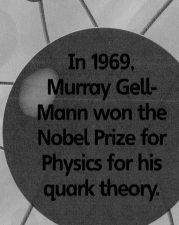

In 1969, Murray Gell-Mann won the Nobel Prize for Physics for his quark theory.

Two Meanings

Gell-Mann borrowed the name "quark" from James Joyce's novel Finnegan's Wake. In the novel, the phrase "three quarks" has two meanings. It sometimes refers to Mr. Finnegan's three children. It also refers to Mr. Finnegan himself. In the same way, a quark is a separate, independent particle. It also composes a larger particle, such as a proton or neutron.

Glossary

anion A negatively charged ion

archaeologist A person who studies fossils, ancient peoples, and other things to understand past human life

atomic number The number of protons in the nucleus of an atom

bond The means by which atoms, ions, or groups of atoms are held together

cation A positively charged ion

chemical property How a material reacts with other materials

chemical reaction A change that produces one or more new substances

compound A substance made of two or more different types of atoms

covalent compound Atoms of different elements that share electrons

current A stream of electrical charge

decay To begin to decompose

electrolysis Producing chemical changes by passing an electric current through a conductor

electron A tiny, negatively charged particle

element A material made from only one kind of atom

fractional Fairly small

gravity A force of attraction between particles that happens because of their mass

ignite To catch fire

ion An atom or a group of atoms with an electric charge

ionic compound An atom that has lost an electron

isotope An atom that belongs to the same element but has a different number of neutrons

kinetic energy Energy associated with motion

mass A quantity of matter that holds together

mass number The number of protons and neutrons in the nucleus of an atom

matter Anything that occupies space and has mass

miner A person who digs pits or tunnels from which minerals are taken

molecule Two or more atoms held together by chemical bonds

neutron A tiny particle with no charge

nuclear fission A type of nuclear reaction in which a neutron splits the nucleus of a large atom

nuclear fusion A nuclear reaction in which heavier nuclei are built from lighter nuclei, releasing huge amounts of energy

nucleus The center of an atom

orbital A circle that makes up a path for an electron

particle accelerator A device used to study the nucleus of an atom

physical properties A characteristic that can be seen or measured without changing what a material is made of

proton A tiny, positively charged particle

quark A fundamental particle of matter

radiation Energy given off in the form of waves or particles

radioactive Describing something that gives off radiation

reactive Tending to react

repel Keep away

shell A framework or structure

state of matter Whether something is a sold, a liquid, or a gas

subatomic particle The particle inside an atom

tracing Following or studying

turbine An engine with blades that spin around from the pressure of water, steam, or air

unstable Readily changing

Index

Web Finder

www.chem4kids.com/files/atom_intro.html
americanhistory.si.edu/kids/molecule/
library.thinkquest.org/J001539/
www.cambridgephysics.com/
www.webelements.com

www.chemistry.mcmaster.ca/bader/aim/
library.thinkquest.org/3659/atommole/
education.jlab.org/qa/atom_idx.html
www.edinformatics.com/il/il_chem.htm
csep10.phys.utk.edu/astr162/lect/light/atoms.html